Father to Son

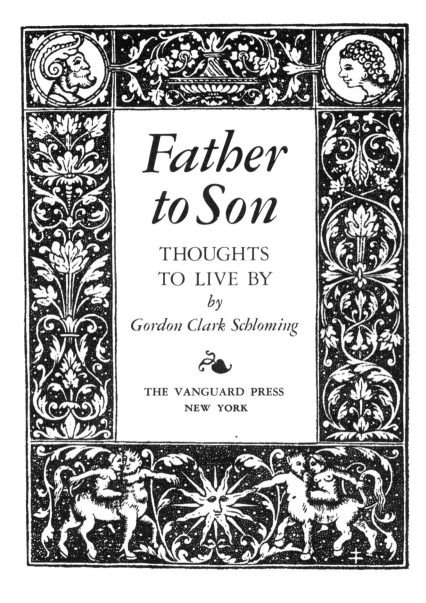

Father to Son

THOUGHTS
TO LIVE BY

by

Gordon Clark Schloming

THE VANGUARD PRESS
NEW YORK

For my wife, Jennifer,
who shares in the work

ACKNOWLEDGMENTS

Illustrations are taken, with gratitude
for their mastery and imagination, from
Albrecht Dürer, Martin Schongauer, and
other old masters. My thanks also to
Tom Torre Bevans for the design, typography,
and general creative contributions.

CONTENTS

He who sets out to banish
all evil in the world
forgets the portion within himself
and commits a slow, unwitting suicide.

1 *My Dear Son*

ou have inquired lately of how I came to live my life as I did, and what it was that guided me along the way. Of course, it is common curiosity for a youth about to embark on adult adventures to ask his elders if there are any magic formulas for deciphering the mysteries of life. I take your inquiry as a sign of my age rather than my wisdom. In truth, I have few answers, as the mistakes in my own life will well attest. But I have pondered your questions nonetheless, and offer you these pieces of commonplace advice. These thoughts began as conversations with myself. I have extended them, as an indulgence of old age, in an attempt to set my mind straight, now that I have passed over much of my rather crooked path. I share them with you in the hope that your journey may have fewer false turns and a greater sense of satisfaction at its end.

Since you are just at an age to set out in conscious search of yourself, you will come shortly to appreciate how much of your person is composed of the various parts you play in a collective drama, and how much of the script you write yourself. Much of the advice I give you is designed to nourish the playwright in you. With thoughtfulness and courage, you will manage to discover your unique character and mark out areas where you intend to make your own special contribution. No doubt when you reach this point you will find some of my advice a trifle ridiculous: this will attest your independence. In the meantime, I hope it will be a point of departure for your personal voyage of discovery until you can take guidance from your own vision of things.

Please remember that your individual identity takes much by inheritance from your family. I have presumed upon these family feelings to try to share some of my hard-earned sentiments about what makes a good life. You may firmly reject such advice as old-fashioned— which may be both the folly and the freedom of the young. But you will ply your new trade with old tools, fashioned in the family, though tempered by your own experience. Among these tools, if we are worth anything at all, you will find a sense of abiding values from which to draw spiritual sustenance. To be sure, this family legacy, freighted with confining expectations and established answers, will leave you at times frustrated and defeated. But it is a legacy that provides continuity, purpose, and a sense of place that you will need in times of trial and personal disorientation. These roots will retain their vitality if you nourish them, through your own growth, in ways that make a contribution to the whole. The connectedness of generations depends on your putting enough faith in community that you retain respect for basic values, while remaking obsolete institutions to suit new times and new needs.

So I send you out to plant your own seeds. You will cultivate them with joy, water them with tears, and they will, I am sure, bear fruit, though you may sweat mightily in the making. Perhaps in a moment of rest, you will take out this little almanac of advice, so you may know better which way the wind is blowing and where most likely to plant, that you may get sun and sweet fruit rather than barrenness and bitterness. At the least, when you are well-established and your own enterprises are thriving luxuriously, it will afford you a little amusement and the recollection that you remain always in my loving thoughts.

2 *How to Say Hello*

A smile can enliven,
amuse, even conquer—
but it should hide nothing.

The most remarkable awkwardness occurs in routine encounters between strangers, due chiefly to the unwillingness of one person to acknowledge, freely and directly, the presence of another. This is a particularly severe problem when children meet adults or when persons of one sex encounter the other. Much stammering, painful silence, and lonely hours can be avoided by following a few simple practices. You risk nothing with a frank hello. Some persons will avoid approaching anyone, standing on ceremony, modesty, or deference. Others enjoy the power they think they get by being greeted first by another. Reject all such nonsense. It is sufficiently difficult to communicate with another, even one long familiar, that I think it quite unnecessary to burden encounters with elaborate rituals. Think, too, of the number of shy violets who, for the sake of appearances, cast their eyes aside, sitting demure and silent in a painful (and lonely) propriety, and then have to settle for the butcher or the boy next door. Treat a friendly hello as a gift and give it freely. The following guidelines may prove helpful:

1. When you enter a room, greet everyone and acknowledge each person's presence with a handshake, a touch, a smile, a word, a name if you know it. Such a pleasure it is to ratify in some small symbolic way that you are in touch with everyone!

2. Greet *everyone* without exception, including the dog.

3. When saying hello, stand tall, look the person in the eye, and try to see what is unique about him and the mood in which he offers himself to you. Children in particular should heed this advice and avoid the appearance that they need apologize for their presence.

4. Special directness is required when presenting yourself to someone whose favor you particularly covet, namely, a prospective patron or someone whose affection you seek in the hope of an intimate relationship. These are times that invite every sort of ruse and calculation in the expectation that you may be made less vulnerable or that the situation can be turned more certainly to your advantage. I advise avoiding all such pretense, since you will be unmasked soon enough. Learn

to like who you are and have confidence that you will be accepted by others. There is nothing that will win affection more quickly than a confident spirit created by your own forthrightness.

20

3 *On Saying Good-by*

The chief problem in leave-taking is that it takes too long, considering how much goes unsaid. This is due to a maddening quality common to all poignant but fleeting moments—the emotions multiply in direct proportion to the scarcity of available time. I offer this consolation: no matter how much time may be suddenly yours by the grace of some guardian angel, you will still fail to say all that you feel you must. Consequently, the important things must already have been said. Do not wait until good-by to declare yourself; do it now. If you have been genuine, direct, and generous in your praise, your lover will then already know that among all things, she stands most dear. Your host, too, will already know that his hearth is as warm as his heart. If you have not made these things clear in the course of daily events, your good-by, no matter how eloquent, will be small recompense. So the old saying, "short and sweet," should inform you in your farewells above all other things.

Reflection also tells us that good advice in small things acquires even more weight in matters more grave. How easy it is to quit the table and take leave of your compatriots at the tavern. Even a summer friend takes a minimum of tears. But to quit your family and make your way in the world—that is the most difficult farewell of all! Yet it too must not be prolonged. Whoever hangs on too long, parent or child, will find himself diminished and confused. Indeed, each situation in life, great or small, has its time that must not be overstayed. If you enter each opportunity, each relationship with abandon and give it something substantial of yourself, when the good-by comes, you can accept it with calm and the assurance that what you have lost in the last good-by is to be found again in the next hello.

23

4 *How to Behave in New Surroundings*

I n any unfamiliar setting the first question we ask is, "What should I do? How should I behave?" And the uncertainty we confront commonly makes us afraid. For dealing with your fears, I recommend a careful study of the deer, who in such a matter seems so wise, though we so carelessly classify him among the "inferior" beings. When startled or caught in a strange encounter, a deer will become perfectly still and display the most remarkable alertness to all around him. Nothing escapes his notice. He is patient and confident, awaiting a clear sign that will determine his direction or purpose. He has learned the secret of responding to the compelling event. If he had dashed off at the first instant, he may well have leaped directly into

the puma's path. So, like the deer, I advise you to wait, watch, and attune yourself to what is around you.

I recommend only this difference: take it as a general rule that unknown situations invite adventure, not danger, and strive to be open to each new experience. In social settings, respond above all to the people, since human qualities are both the most important and the most universal. One last caution: the novice or the stranger will often search frantically for the formal code of behavior and conform slavishly to what he guesses to be the prevailing custom or manner. Such a tactic is folly, since it compounds fear and encourages a foolish imitation of tradition that in a newcomer is either inappropriate or offensive. Give yourself time to

learn the lore; then you can respect it. Until then, be
yourself, trust your intuition, and hang the rules. More

often than not, your hosts will be happy to dispense with the formalities as well.

5

How to Judge Another and When You Should Not

Men may live by rules or by their ambitions, but the best live by the principles of love.

ood judgment, especially of persons, is one of life's most valuable tools. It will always assure you of having worthy and faithful friends. However, if you judge too harshly or in a condescending manner, you will have no friends at all. Play God, and you will be, by definition, alone. When you judge someone, judge for yourself, not for everyone or for all time. If you are to take the measure of a man, weigh his substance, not his aspect, for appearances weigh nothing. Contrary to the popular saying, clothes do not make the man. Have we not heard of the pauper who inherited riches because he gave the beggar/king kindness rather than contempt? Or of another king who set such store in the opinion of others (rather than his own good judgment) that he paraded about, not in rags, but in nothing at all? A man who has not cultivated his own good judgment is always at the mercy of another's. So take advice, but do not be tyrannized by it, and if you wish advice, take it from someone you can trust. For me, signs of one worthy of trust are these:

1. He will look you in the eye.

2. He will have a sense of humor. I take this to be a particularly important measure of any man who

holds public office, since the affairs of the nation will quickly confound or possess a man who cannot laugh, especially at his own mistakes.

3. He conducts every relationship in a spirit of reciprocity, asking not more than he is himself willing to give. Such an attitude is essential if a man with many successes is to cultivate his character, for only thus will he acquire a sense of stewardship in proportion to his accomplishments.

4. He will have an essential humility. By this I mean the capacity to accept persons quite unlike himself and value their company for the very qualities he himself lacks.

5. He will possess a largeness of soul that recognizes that some things will always escape his powers of reason, and some things *should* always escape his control.

6. He is not afraid to say: "I don't know."

7. He knows himself, or if he becomes momentarily confused, he will not trample over you in his search for himself.

8. Somewhere, sometime, he has learned to love someone profoundly.

Having offered these rules as general guides, let me add a few footnotes. Try to govern all of your relationships by a spirit of forgiveness. This protects against your own bad judgment and also provides for the fact that people and circumstances change quite beyond our initial expectations. Do not give up a friend merely because he has disappointed you. If the friendship is unworthy, he will, by his bad faith, destroy it; you, in your haste, need not. Finally, there are circumstances where you must avoid passing judgments of any kind:

1. When you are in a new setting or foreign culture with which you are unfamiliar.

2. When you have made a mistake that you recognize but refuse to accept. Make restitution, but do not indulge in self-recrimination. How much more worthy to spend your energy avoiding the next mistake than compounding the last.

3. When dealing with matters of faith or deep personal belief, as long as the consequences of such beliefs are confined to a private domain.

4. When you have fallen in love, and then finally fallen out.

6

On the Folly of Shams, Masks, and Games

*A white lie is a black
one painted to
impress the neighbors.*

ersons of good sense will avoid pretense like the plague, since a sickness of the spirit is the certain result. We have only to ask, why is it that someone will give great energy to an arrogant or silly masquerade? Clearly, because he is afraid he will appear quite naked and unacceptable if clothed in the common and seeming scanty garb of his everyday being. But masks and games are feeble defenses that deceive others only for a few moments, though we may deceive ourselves for a lifetime. Thus, the game-playing masquerader is condemned to a succession of superficial encounters, enduring each round of boring banter with the thought that he is, after all, part of such a *grande scène*. But if he meets a delightful woman, dare he take off his mask to kiss her? Will she know him or like him when he calls upon her after the ball? Too often the clever schemer is caught in his own devices and either cannot abandon his role when he would like to step off the stage, or is unmasked, with embarrassing results, at the most vulnerable and inopportune moment. To be sure, there are some who, through art, industry, and considerable intelligence may become quite successful (in worldly terms) by the cleverness and wit with which they create a public persona. These are the familiar politicians, salesmen, and celebrities. They set their stock in power, fame, and fortune, which is surely valued by many. But I say to you that these men gamble with fools' gold. How much better to use your wit to delight rather than deceive. How much better to use your intelligence to enlighten rather than enslave. How much better to have a self-esteem founded in a solid reputation among friends than leave one's sense of worth to the public whim. Those who are compelled to take on airs display a terrible insecurity and will sooner or later, noses in the air, stumble. They have not the capacity to see clearly who they really are and where they are going.

So must the sincere and earnest man forswear games of any sort? Is there no mirth or levity in the land? I answer, yes, but the test of a good game is that it serve one of two ends. It must be for amusement and diversion, which means that everyone present must play and the game continues at no one's expense. Or it must be a game that heals, that has as its object the greater enlightenment, awareness, or well-being of another, as when a parent, teacher, or physician adopts a role that may lead his charge by an indirect path to a more perfect place.

7

How to Know
Your Own Mind

ne of the most difficult tasks we face daily is that of making up our minds. Each day, for as long as you live, you will be faced with choices. These choices represent your opportunities in life, but also the special burden of your individuality. Such choices become increasingly difficult if you fail to know yourself and to cultivate the art of choosing well. How many times have you conversed in confusion with a companion over which entertainment you should attend? How often have you sat bewildered in a tavern, struggling at length with your selection of victuals, and then succumbed in the end to the exact choice of your neighbor? Think of the number of arguments (maybe even marriages) that could be saved if those in conflict would figure out what they truly do think or want. It is important to realize that decisions give you the power to create order in your life. Decisions also require you to say good-by to some-

thing; that is why they are hard to make. The price of order is not being able to do everything you want. Successful decisions require a clear sense of priorities, purposes, or basic values, and the courage to give yourself wholeheartedly to the path you have chosen. Second-guessing yourself is the surest road to disaster and should be avoided at all costs. Second-guessing, however, is not to be confused with changing your mind, which requires the greatest courage of all. If you refrain from a clear choice, hoping to husband your alternatives and save the pain, Time will steal all your choices and you will have to do what Fate decrees, like it or not.

If you seek relief from the burden of choice, take hope in two thoughts:

1. There is almost always more than one good alternative. Life is rich in spite of the fact that the stinginess of Time requires us to choose. If there is poverty, it is most often in our imagination and our unwillingness to accept the many routes to our preferred destination. An ingenious (and patient) pathfinder will often discover the right road, whichever way he may have gone.

2. A good routine is worth a thousand bad decisions. Some decisions are sufficiently small in their consequences that they are not worth making more than once. These should be relegated to the realm of habit. So, too, there are decisions that will invite such conflict that it takes all your powers of resolve to come to a satisfactory conclusion. These occur most often in the largest and most central areas of life and love. These decisions can also acquire a binding power if placed in the matrix of a routine—by which I mean a commitment to make the same decision every day for a lifetime. Marriage particularly profits from just such a routine, which is the best protection against the childish impulse we all possess to want everything.

One final piece of advice: knowing your mind at any moment is made vastly easier if you study your feelings carefully. Too often we are so fixed on the signposts and billboards at each intersection that we forget to consult the little signs within. If you are attentive, you will find them: a flushed face, a turn of the stomach, a twitching eye, a small and unexpected smile, the urge to flee, a pressure in the loins, a pain in the chest. These are signs that will warn you dependably about the rocks in the road (and, if you have rushed off in an ill-considered direction, in your head). You need not be invariably ruled by them, but you ignore them at your peril! The test of a sound decision is the freedom you feel when it is made.

8

Petrugnus biß vins nit zuschwer. Die frongkhait schleffe ein langzeit her.
Ernacht sy, es wurt dir zuschwer.

How to Choose a Career

he amount of advice a young man can receive on his prospective career is legion. Many will advise you to go where the money is. From my point of view, money will make you a living but never a career. Nor will it ever, by itself, make you happy. Others will say to watch the market and go where the opportunities are greatest. If our world were, by some happy coincidence, organized in such a way that professions with greatest promise rendered service in areas of greatest need, I would judge this good advice. Unhappily, we often need most what people least want to pay for (or, as with love, cannot pay for). Finally, there is friendly parental advice. Unfortunately, parents seem either to want for you whatever they, by bad luck or their own limits, could not get, or to expect that your feet should fit just fine in father's shoes. If you pick either path, pre-

pare to carry your parents with you, for they will always be on your back. My advice is to do what you *love*. Usually this is also that for which you are most fit. If circumstances do not provide such a chance, then do what you must. By the latter I mean, take what you can to sustain a livelihood, but give your work where you see a need. The sense of fulfillment that comes from such a mission of service will more than compensate for a meager income or a sense that your talents are misplaced. If you are needed, then your efforts, however fumbling, are never wasted. If at last you still feel a calling for work that does not pay, make it a hobby and do it for free.

9 *On the Meaning of Education*

veryone has told you by now of the inestimable value of a good education. I myself have, from time to time, given you books that amused me or provoked me in the hope that they would cultivate in you the love of good literature and the breadth of knowledge that mark the educated man. Still, the best years of your education are ahead of you (this seems always to be so), and will require great energy and proper orientation if you are to avoid becoming frustrated or bored. The first thing you must understand is that your teachers, being generally knowledgeable, serve as rich sources of useful information. To secure it, however, you must

*A man is marked as educated
not by his complicated answers but
by his clear, simple questions.*

be prepared always to ask questions without the slight-est hesitation. In my experience, the quality and excite-ment of the answer are in direct proportion to the thoughtfulness, simplicity, and daring of the question.

A few teachers, if you are lucky, will also be for you examples of the inquiring mind at work. These lat-ter are precious, for they can help you acquire a set of intellectual tools that will serve you a lifetime, and pro-vide the motivation to use them besides. But the ordinary teacher can be expected to school you in a subject; if you wish to be truly educated, you must consequently depend on yourself. If you complain that school is uninteresting or irrelevant, or that it teaches conformity and merely trains you to fill a place in society, it is because you let it do so. Often this results from wanting too much to please the professor or your parents, and caring too little to please yourself. It is an unhappy truth that anyone who depends solely on others for the test of his achievements will end life feeling he has accomplished nothing: there are so many to please and someone is always dissatisfied. So set your own sights and, provided you give your best effort, you can feel free to demand that your teachers teach you what you want to know. If there is no one in school with such an interest, find him in the world and make yourself an eager apprentice. Anyone who loves his work makes a fine teacher if you have but eyes to see and ears to listen.

If by this route your education takes place outside the confines of the classroom, you still must not scoff at the scholarly world, for you will never escape the necessity of consulting the written word. Books are the swiftest, simplest method of sharing the wealth of the world's collected knowledge, whether you are interested in the wisdom of the ages or practical techniques for surviving in the work-a-day world. No matter how skilled your teachers, they will never substitute for sitting down with a book and digging in. As a strategy for reading intelligently, I recommend that you always begin with a question, if no more than to ask what you expect to learn from the book and what is the perspective from which the author presents his ideas. For myself, I always write profusely in the margins. This saves me much exclaiming and swearing aloud (which librarians seem not to care for, no matter the enthusiasm for learning it may display). It also leaves me in the end with not one book, but two. By this means you will discover that every book starts with an idea, an implied question, the quest for a personal answer. The author's result is, of course, only one among many. If you respond freely to his ideas as you read, you will discover these other possibilities between the lines, which give you a better understanding of the uniqueness of his answer and a chance to frame your own. Otherwise you become a mere prisoner of the ideas you happen to be reading at the moment.

If you come to books in this manner, you will end up an educated man, no matter how meager your classroom opportunities or how poor the official reports. On the other hand, if your intelligence and industry lead you to the heights of academic achievement, you will still retain an essential humility and tolerance for the views of others. If you respect the diversity of possible answers, you will perceive how another, in good faith, can find his way to a conflicting result without being thought a dullard or a nincompoop. Then you can understand that he simply began with a different question than yours, viewed his subject from a different perspective, and consequently sees, in truth, something new. At best, you can appreciate that learning is not a lonely or a competitive enterprise, but an essentially cooperative one. Such cooperation will encourage creative conflict, preserve the dialectic of question and answer, and teach you that Truth is better illuminated by shedding more light on the subject than can come from your own little candle.

You will teach more in a single smile than an hour-long lesson: humor cuts the edges off abstract ideas and makes us eager to receive them.

10 *On the Power of Words*

and When to Keep Still

He who lives on promises.
he cannot keep eats
his own words, and is
filled with emptiness.

ords have power in a double sense: by the power of the impression they convey and by the power of the promise they keep. Others will first judge the quality of your mind and manners by how they are displayed in your speech. If your education has served you well, it will have honed your wits and made keen your powers of expression, that your presence may be incisive in first impressions. The latter have no value in themselves, but they are the means by which you come quickly to be trusted and taken seriously. On a first encounter, your words have the power to put others at ease and assure them of your good will, substance, and sound judgment. These qualities are your keys for opening doors to new friendships.

These impressions will gain the weight of reputation also by the power of your word: by how carefully you keep faith with others. Empty promises sow bitterness and reap scorn and neglect. If you bend ears with idle talk, you may as well box them, for they will soon be closed to you. Those who can be relied on to match words with action will be sought out as worthy friends by everyone. Indeed, if you have any hope of wielding influence over others or playing a weighty role in community affairs, you must learn to speak your mind effectively. Great leaders are those who communicate ideas to the minds of others. Theirs is not the coercive power of chains but the inspiration of ideas uncaged. They have discovered how to capture complex matters in a simple phrase that will move the masses. Never underestimate the power of an idea, well placed and well put.

More important than their public impact, however, is the power of words to put your mind at peace. Stammering, awkward phrases, inappropriate words, mute moments will leave you frustrated that you cannot make yourself understood to others. Your head will ache with unborn ideas. Becoming articulate will set you free to thrive in any group of people with the self-assurance of clarity and directness in your conversation. Nothing is quite as intense or exciting as an exchange between persons who delight in words and have the knack of banishing confusion or bringing amusement by the choice of words that say something just so. Develop this skill and you will never be bored, for you will have discovered that good conversation is the height of all entertainment.

Still, there are times when words fail, or at least when wisdom warrants keeping quiet. Among many such circumstances I shall list a few that they may serve as guides to the sanctity of silence. Keep still on these occasions:

1. When you have just asked a question and are tempted to supply the answer yourself. This will teach you to substitute real questions for rhetorical ones.

2. When your spouse, lover, or friend cries. Wait, for words will not spare their weeping. They cry because they have been trying to say something they could not tell, or you would not hear.

3. When confronting a zealot or a doting relative, neither of whom has learned to listen.

4. When children chatter or play tricks merely to capture your attention. If their hijinks are harmless, follow the principle that naughty children are best ignored.

5. When trying to comfort another from an inconsolable loss. Hold them, be with them, but save your breath. At such a time a loving look and a quiet but constant presence are worth more than a mountain of words that change nothing.

6. When you want especially to be heard. By this I mean that any speech profits from the opportunity to collect your thoughts quietly in advance, and resonates in direct proportion to the length of silence that precedes it.

7. When you walk in nature.

8. When you talk from fear of the silence.

11 *On Insecurity*

> *Grasp fear as*
> *fodder for growth.*

ll of us are insecure; only madmen and children have the innocence to act without reflection or care for consequences. Insecurity is in this sense the companion of conscience. Find me a perfectly fearless man and I will show you a fanatic or someone without scruples of any kind. What marks men out as different is how they manage to deal with their fears. A man of character learns to admit his fears and acquires the humility to ask for help in overcoming them. Facing a fear allows you to inspect it and see it for what it really is. If you mask your fear, it will return to haunt you in a thousand disguises.

Insecurity is camouflaged in three common ways: in affability, appetite, and affluence. Have you not met these men who display an endless string of smiles? You would think they are trying to sell you something! In fact they are trying to sell themselves on their own acceptability, and you become an accomplice in their great quest to assassinate the self-critical spirit within. Men often eat indulgently to feel full, because their insecurities make them feel empty. What more symbolic way to appear substantial when you fear you are worth nothing? As for money, it is used as the one great substitute for all unsatisfied needs, to pay the unmet emotional bills. Fearing rejection, the materialist buries himself in an avalanche of things and clings to them like rocks—anchors against a lonely existence. This urge to acquisition seems to lie in not feeling loved. Whoever collects friends like coins, or becomes infatuated with wealth itself, is seeking acceptance by indirect means. In every case, the answer is to seek security within, and to give your love utterly without restraint or calculation.

One final remark about money: If you earn much of it, take it as a gift and learn to spend it well. A mere bauble that breaks tomorrow, if bought with a child's delight, will be worth its price, so long as the money was not marked for the expense of your basic sustenance. A purchase bought in a grudging spirit, on the other hand, no matter how essential or extravagant, will never make you happy. Money gives pleasure as much by the spirit in which it is spent as by the object it acquires.

60

12 *On Anger*

Anger, unexpressed, echoes.

hen angry, you can choose to express it, control it, transform it, or make it righteous, but you will never succeed in ignoring it. It is said that a good man, rather than exact a narrow, vengeful justice at the expense of a misguided enemy, will turn the other cheek. If you have the courage, do so, and you will have won the moral terrain and a victory over yourself. But do not pretend that you have not been wronged or hurt. It is one thing to renounce retribution, but quite another to renounce your feelings altogether. Give justice to your enemy but do justice to yourself as well. Do not spare him your angry daggers only to turn them within. Squash your aggressive action, but not your anger, for it will be banished only to return again and plague you in subtle ways. Kept within, it will eat at you like a fox at your heart. Swallowed whole while yet alive, your anger will sprout in secret or surprising ways, its force redoubled from incubating in quiet anguish. Better to be mad in the moment than become mad in that slow, stifling manner you cannot escape.

But you may say to me: "I have no right to be angry with him." I say, that is for your antagonist to judge, not you. Say what you feel and if you are mistaken, he will show you soon enough how falsely you judge. Then if your anger be petty and undeserved, give it up as freely as you gave it to him in the first place. But if you refuse to examine your anger, then you become its agent, not its owner, and it will push you around like a drunk judge before a hanging jury. If you will not discuss what hurts you, how can there be a cure? If you feel wronged, but fake compliance, whom have you fooled but yourself? The only way to dispel uncomfortable feelings is to find them and claim them as your own, to take them out of the air and attach them to something real. Otherwise they foul the atmosphere, sensed but unseen, and are utterly immune to investigation. The great mystery is that anger's power is purged through its expression, and no love is so sweet as that which follows on a good spat.

But expressing anger openly and claiming your feelings are only first steps. Most important is the exercise in self-awareness and self-mastery. To be honestly angry, you must know precisely how much of your fury really comes from within, an echo from an old era or a secret way to spite the self. You are freed of such anger in the end, not simply by giving it to another, but by making peace with yourself.

M+S

13 *On Dreams*

n dreams you will find all the lingering parts of your past and premonitions of what is to come. They make up a mystery world of mad logic that contains amazing wisdom if you will but spy a bit through these dirty windows and try to decipher the drama. Onstage, you will find yourself playing all the parts. Listen well, for each actor speaks to you and for you. It is a time for creative conversation with yourself that will save you much muttering during the day. Give attention to your dreams and you will be rewarded, beyond your wildest dreams, with a clear vision of what moves you in your innermost self. Your nightmares tell you of the business in life that you have conducted badly

or left unfinished. Do not fear them: they are tending to a most valuable trash. For these very dreams contain keys to unlock hidden strength for combating your nocturnal demons. Look well at the latter, for when you meet them, metamorphosed, during the day, you will be fighting a more familiar foe, and can use the opportunity to befriend them. Thus, your powers of imagination and insight, your self-knowledge, will be amplified tenfold by even the smallest foray into this shadow world that reflects the substance of life.

So go unafraid, my sweet son, on these nightly journeys into a strange land: take it for a frontier, explore it, make a ready path, clear the thickets, plow and reap, and soon you will be at home.

14 *How to Grow*

Growing up was something that used to happen automatically, but nowadays seems to require instructions. Perhaps this is because we no longer speak of you young people growing as if you had a hand in it yourself; instead, children are being raised these days. It must be that the spirit of modern education has reached right into the home and parents have become frantic studying the latest techniques in child-rearing. This has, no doubt, given to parenting some of the power of modern science. But I still feel a bit like the old farmer: despite all the new-fangled equipment and information, I know a lot depends on the quality of the seed, the luck of the weather, and the grace of God. So we still raise our

To grow in stature
you have only to eat,
but to grow in spirit,
you must chew on things a bit.

offspring in perpetual fear of crop failure! This being
so, an old-timer's lore seems as sound as any. Here is one
recipe I recollect for raising a sturdy crop:

1. Set the seeds down in fertile soil.
2. Water frequently with praise and love.
3. Cultivate with care and consideration.
4. Stand them in the sunshine of your smiles.
5. Weed tenderly, but often, that you need not pull up so
   much at one time.
6. Do not pick their fruit while green; it must ripen in
   its own time, that it may suit the greengrocer, not
   the gardener.

7. When you have done with the basics, leave well enough alone; fussing with them makes them wilt.
8. When they bear fruit, do not be overproud of your efforts; let them take the credit while you tend to a new garden.

But I have quite forgotten myself, giving you advice for which you have no use, at least for a good long

while. Perhaps I suffer that tendency of many old folks to amuse themselves with the sound of their own voices, and to offer up all the old advice that went unused in their own youth. For you, I reckon, the task is not how to be a parent, but how to deal with parents and with yourself as you grow up. The best bet is to believe in yourself, since you have no one else, in the final account, to depend on. Learn your strengths and your weaknesses, trust the first and learn to tolerate the second. In your

search, we as parents can help, but at some point you must set out on your own ventures. Resist us if we try to lead you everywhere by the nose. When you are old enough not to heed unquestioningly, you are old enough to take some responsibility to think for yourself. The law may insist that this occurs at eighteen or twenty years of age, but I recall it happening at three or four. In any event, if you have an opinion, no one can deny your right to it, so stand up for what you think. Parents should be respected but never worshiped, since you will soon enough find our feet of clay have muddied your own foundation. And when you start to sink a bit, you will have to build again for yourself. To set the pillars of a self-sufficient structure on solid ground, you must avoid the quicksands of excessive pride or morbid self-chastisement. Avoid becoming so sure of yourself that you resist anything new in life, or so immobilized by fear that you have not the resilience or initiative to try again if you fail. Growing up is, by its essence, a process of adaptation.

*Development, in a nation
or a woman, entails a
redistribution of resources.*

15

On Letter Writing

ince you are someone with talent, industry, and a taste for adventure, you will sooner or later move from your boyhood home. If you wish to keep your friends and a sense of family, you will have to learn how to write letters. This is, speaking frankly, one of the tasks of good living that I have not yet mastered. As I see it, the largest obstacle to faithful correspondence is the lack of an immediate face-to-face relationship. Thus, letter writing is one of several important areas where we must learn to defer immediate gratification and make an investment. Family and old friends are investments that are well worth the effort. A second obstacle is to become so overwhelmed by the desire to say everything that you end up writing nothing. Avoid the newsy, chit-chat letter that tells your friends all about the weather but naught about you. But do write! Write something short, simple, substantial, and write often. If it is a particularly old and close friendship, it will thrive like a weed, unattended for a time. But even weeds must be watered, and most of us are more fragile flowers and require more regular nourishment. A letter is a gift of light and love, and nothing enlivens a day more than a few words from afar.

I add this: a letter is no substitute for a renewed presence and shared times together. Letters keep your friendships from fading, but if you want them to grow, attend them in person. This last advice is particularly important for young lovers; those who accumulate large stacks of love letters seem by some unfailing law to end up burning them.

16

A Few Essential Rules for the Good Guest

1. When you are dining in company, accept whatever is put upon your plate and eat it thankfully. If the food is strange, take it as an adventure. If it is familiar but disliked, ask for a small portion. But refuse nothing and eat all you take.

2. Do not, however, take a second portion merely to appear grateful or gracious. Nor should you refuse another helping out of politeness. If your host offers food out of form alone, you will have the pleasure of making him an honest man and breaking him of a bad habit.

3. Do not allow yourself to be waited on hand and foot. If your stay is extensive, there are many tasks you can take up in return for your host's generosity: dishes to wash, wood to chop, a fence to mend, a bed to make, a bit of bread to buy, a child who needs watching, or a witty story.

P. BRVEGEL. INVENT   ALIX

80

4. Avoid activities that engage some members of the household at the expense of others. It is ill-mannered to indulge a sphinx-like game of chess before the fire when the clan has gathered to chat. A boisterous round of beer and cards among the men, while the ladies slave like charwomen, will not bring you a ready welcome on a return visit, whatever the man of the house may say in his merriment.

5. Be aware whether the circumstances of your visit are happy or not, and judge the length of your stay accordingly. Your host may have extended a well-intentioned invitation but hit on hard times in the meanwhile.

6. Do not perpetuate an arrangement where you are always the guest. If you cannot invite others to share your own hospitality, accept invitations with care. Never let the poverty of your circumstances prevent you from inviting people into your home—it is not your wealth you are sharing, but your good will. If you are a traveler in a foreign land and cannot return the hospitality, endeavor to find ways to give while you are yet receiving; a bottle of wine bought for the occasion; a song, entertainment, or talent you may share; a book you have finished but they may yet enjoy; or any other small way of enriching their day by your presence among them.

17 *How to Be with Children*

hildren are a constant delight and good teachers besides. They show us how we really are as human beings. Children teach us that we are cruel, but also free, and that nothing will serve us so well as a good imagination. Think what ingenuity is displayed by the four-year-old who can play happily for hours with two sticks and a rock. If we showed such resourcefulness as adults, would we ever be bored? How much we have to learn also from that wonderful fantasy world children inhabit in those magic years. They are supremely curious and have, happily enough, not yet learned to shun the question that betrays ignorance, as if it were bad. They see everything that goes on around them and respond with a directness and honesty that is disarming. They are fearless, utterly without false modesty, and eager beyond belief. Find a child who is not so and you will find parents who have not love enough between them to make it so. To be sure, an infant can be arbitrary, petulant, or full of fear; but more often than not he has been schooled to be so, little monkey that he is, by having absolute apes for parents. Most babies cry only when they really need something. Would it be so bad a world if adults could manage, with unashamed tears, to do the same? Childishness finds favor nowhere, but child-likeness is the very root of life—lose it and you have lost the capacity to become new again.

If you want to inhabit a child's world for a few happy hours and to be made welcome by him, I suggest the following:

1. When you approach a child, stoop to converse, so you seem not too tall. Talking to a giant is intimidating. Besides, we all need to practice getting on our knees now and then.
2. Speak softly and touch gently so that you do not frighten unnecessarily.
3. Treat the youngster as a separate being with a space of his own and trespass not. Visit by permission and he will come to you in his own time.
4. Recognize him as a child, but talk with him like an adult. He can reason and, even when very young, understand. What he fails to grasp in your words he will catch in your manner, your tone of voice. Not one whit will be added by babbling in a baby-talk language you do not understand.

5. Approach him in the spirit of play, laugh a lot, and leave your own heavy games at home. He has no use for sternness, bullying, or a pompous and aloof sobriety. Nor does he need to be tutored too early in adult games—he will learn them soon enough.
6. Be consistent—it is the surest mark of your adultness —but do not expect it in a child, who is, after all, experimenting in life.
7. Do not confuse love with indulgence. There is no tyrant worse than a child who knows he is in control.

If you keep the above matters in mind, you will also get good practice at being a parent, since only good habits will save you from the upheaval brought on by your own children.

18 *On the Importance*
of Discipline

he Greeks hailed the value of the golden
mean, which we have taken to be some mellow middle
ground that is gained through temperance, compromise,
and the cultivation of an attitude of repose. A balanced
life requires each of these, but is gained above all
through discipline. This explains, without doubt, why
that ancient people appreciated equally the rigors of
philosophy and athletics. You could do no better than to
emulate them, making body and mind at once supple and
strong.

Discipline lends order to all things. To love it
lends steadfastness: your wife will weep, feeling un-
loved, if you allow disarray in work or leisure to steal
moments that were meant for her. In the creative arts,
discipline harnesses our powers and makes them potent.
The musician must know his scales before he can ascend
to expressive heights. It is that marvelous blend of passion and control that lends all art its essential grace and

Keep but half your resolves and
you will have twice what you need to be happy.

beauty. So, too, in child-rearing, discipline makes your brood well-bred. It provides limits for a child who by nature knows no bounds. Only thus will a child acquire a sense of justice, which is knowing that he is only one among many, that each has his place and yet each must give another his due.

If too little discipline yields young men who are unmolded monsters, too much can create mannequins. Discipline itself requires a limit, which is provided by an unfailing awareness of your purpose. Every regimen, every rule must take its direction from an immediate aim; otherwise you spend your time shooting arrows at the stars. No one is quicker to sniff out a punishment without purpose than a child facing a parent who has retreated to the rules. If you cannot explain why to a child, then say yes, and spare the rod. Parents who resort arbitrarily to their authority perpetuate a mean and petty breed. Promote justice in your home and you will need neither parliaments nor armies to protect democracy in the land. Further, avoid companions who find an end in the discipline itself, for they possess caged and tormented imaginations, or a disguised will to power. They are trying to tame the beasts within or have become infatuated with the experience of control itself. To be disciplined does not mean to be driven, though ambition and fear serve as common counterfeits. If these become directing forces in your life, you become enslaved by unyielding taskmasters who impose demands contrary to a contented and well-ordered life. Finally, remember this: every discipline is meant to be discarded when it has accomplished its end and thereby outlived its usefulness.

*A man who cannot
befriend himself
befits no one.*

90

19

On Courage and Honesty as the Main Constituents of Character

I f you are to make your way happily in life, I recommend two qualities that serve as cornerstones for building sound character: courage and integrity. These two are the watchwords of an independent life. Possess these and you will display a radiance that attracts stout friends like moths to a light. They will also create an inner substance that provides backbone, a quiet firmness that sustains you in your solitude or when you find yourself in the dark.

If you wish to be truly courageous, do not follow the example of braggarts and bullies, who think they will be deemed brave by a display of mere bravado. Wait not for heroic times, for courage, to be firm, must be practiced daily. Be courageous in simple ways: speak your mind and speak always the truth. White lies may, after all, be told less to ease the pain for others than for ourselves. In public discourse, be forthright. A retreat from controversy often masquerades as good manners. If there is justice in your stand, defend it. There will always be somebody who will call you impertinent as a means of quieting all protest. He is probably a partner in the present arrangement of things. Never let another reap profit or privilege from your own timidity.

Follow this forthrightness with others by an utter honesty with yourself. To see yourself clearly, with all your faults and flaws, will take the most courage of all. It will protect you, however, from the low estimates of others, since one who is inflated is easily punctured by the barbs of jealous rivals. If you manage courage in this daily battle with yourself and your associates, never retreating faint-heartedly from an honest and forthright manner, you will have won half the battle of being your own man. In this sense, courage is the basis of any act of integrity. It is the outward sign that you have faith in yourself, that there is a light within that illuminates your life.

20 *Twenty Practical Skills*

1. How to sew a button on a shirt.

2. How to cook essential meals.

3. How to plant and tend a garden.

4. How to build a stout, simple structure.

5. How to fix any machine you consider necessary to your mode of living.

6. How to frame a proper letter, with graceful language and good grammar.

7. How to converse in a foreign language.

8. How to carry a tune or play upon an instrument.

9. How to dance.

10. How to paint (at least a house).

Every Man Should Master

11. How to make introductions at a social occasion.

12. How to tell a good story (and know when to stop).

13. How to be silent when you have nothing constructive to say.

14. How to tell someone to his face that you are angry.

15. How to cry.

16. How to say no.

17. How to admit when you are wrong.

18. How to apologize when you are rude.

19. How to quiet a crying child.

20. How to bring home flowers when you are late (and sometimes when you are not).

On Music

usic is like buried treasure: each new piece is a discovery that enriches your life. As a player, you can always find new wealth at your fingertips if you will only dig a bit deeper into the piece. Learning to perform on an instrument is a special delight. It will give you confidence in yourself and a new way to share with another. Yet it also teaches humility, for the best players become so by making themselves perfect stewards, vehicles of the composer's genius and for others windows on a world of sublime harmony. Best of all, music says what is inside when words fail, and lets out what you have locked up within. It speaks to infants and to old folks, to foreigners and friends. It is a gentle medium and a universal language; I advise you to learn it well. Besides, when you are lonely, it is much better than talking to yourself.

22 *About Sex*

ex is a subject that a sensible writer would not touch with a ten-foot pole. I say this not because it is a dirty subject or unfit for discussion. Quite the contrary, there would be no need for advice on sex by so-called experts if it were discussed as a commonplace experience among family and friends. I can give you no better advice than to ask as many questions as possible to inform yourself fully on the subject. Ask without the slightest hesitation, without a pang of guilt, without the least flush in your face, for you have no apology to make over the most common curiosity known to man. You may even, by your frank and unashamed manner, educate your elders to a more healthy attitude. What a wonder it is that in an age of enlightenment we still hold a

*Love is not blind,
it merely has its eyes
firmly fastened on the
most prominent features.*

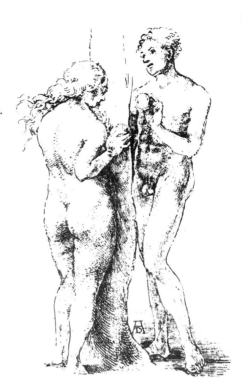

dark shroud over the most universal of human experiences.

I say sex is silly to write about because there is no substitute for experience. No words will prepare you for the power of its pull. No amount of advice will save you from that first elemental fear of failure. No salty old dog can slip you the secrets to amorous success. No tutor can tell you of the supreme, tender bliss of an essentially innocent, unfettered experience. There is little I can tell you to do because good sex is not in the doing but in the feeling, and every man must feel for himself. Indeed, you can avoid abusing yourself and others in sexual matters if you will only pay attention to these feelings and respect them at all times. In circumstances of sexual exploitation, you violate yourself as much as another. Most often this comes from wooing a phantom, who may give you fleeting pleasure, but will not leave you feeling pleased. By phantom I mean the face you put on the real person you are afraid to see. This may be the painted face of someone you think will make you a man. Or it may be the mock look of true love that you lavish on some temporary toy. In either case you are twice fooled: they become pawns in your play, not real people, and you fancy yourself a fine lover without having felt the least bit of love.

To say it simply, there is no substitute for loving each other. Without mutual recognition and love, you are just papièr-maché partners going through the motions: you will have a stiff experience at best. When you are truly in love with someone you can trust, then all fears vanish, all charades cease, and you can count on waking tomorrow with the same woman. Nothing lends passion and abandon to love more than feeling loved. When sex is a genuine and shared experience, you will find more thrill in a taste, a smell, a touch, a look than in all the thousand thrashings (and frequent flops) of fake romance.

One final thought: if you have an urge to power, enter politics, but do not visit it on your lover. Jealousy is an unsavory state of mind, for it marks you as one with the passion to possess, not love. Nothing spoils a love relationship faster than the urge to play parent—that is, to control another. Shun those childish lovers who would make you a parent even in the absence of offspring. They will give you power but they will take everything else, since they refuse to be responsible even for themselves. In short, dependent partners require constant feeding, but cannot fulfill. Marry your match instead, and be happy exercising your power in parliament, not in bed.

23 *On Courtship*

oo young, too long, too far removed—
these are the trials of courtship to which adolescent love
is blind. I know, young man, you will think me foolish
and old-fashioned. I can hear you say to me now: "How
easy it is to referee when you are too old to play the
game. I will wager you did the same things when you
were young. What a tale that old porch swing would tell
if it could talk!" Well, permit me, please, the benefit of
hindsight, that I may spare you the anguish of unre-
quited love.

Few things in life will give you more pain than
to invest great emotion in a girl too young to play a
woman's role. This presumes you know yourself how to
play the man's part. If you are both quite young, forgo
all thoughts of the future. Dally, kiss, while away the
hours, be ardent if you must, but do not make a marriage
out of child's play. The temptation is strong to become
serious too soon: it makes you feel safe, it gives license
to love, it frees you from the trouble of finding others to

fill your time. But the security is false, for few young persons have the resources to create a relationship that will last a lifetime. The promise of love as a license to passion is self-deluding too. If you must be lovers, be so bravely, without the camouflage of pretend promises. If you cannot face your predicament squarely, as frisky creatures, curious, eager, but with little future, then better to wait: you are not old enough to appreciate what you are doing.

It is best if you spend time with several partners, learning what it is like to get along with others. Relationships come in the most remarkable variety—how are you to know what you like if you have not tried a goodly number? Besides, new friends are the best means, bar none, for finding out about yourself. With each new friend you will find new feelings, new ways of being, new parts of yourself. Spend your youth in self-discovery; do not run away from yourself by submitting to a seemingly safe but immature relationship. If you marry your childhood sweetheart, you will remain happy only at the price of remaining dull. Grow or change in the least way and you will be tempted to discard her: your one and only shirt will have shrunk too small. So steer clear of long involvements while you are yet young.

Even less needs to be said regarding the folly of trying to conduct a romance from afar. The best of marriages would not last long if the spouse lived in the next township: most cannot even endure separate bedrooms.

What, then, can explain why two young people insist on conducting a love affair across a continent?

To conclude, I offer a few random hints that may help you through the torments of love in your younger years:

1. *Never* say "I love you" unless you mean it. In fact, let nothing pass your lips you do not firmly believe, especially if you praise her appearance. If a fashion that infatuates her looks ridiculous, tell her so. A lie will only encourage her and condemn you to looking at it daily. If she loves you, she will want an honest evaluation, the better to know how to please you. Whisper sweet nothings to nobody.

2. Be honest in your affection. Do not shrug off her hand or kiss merely because you are in a public place. If your manly image is endangered, change your definition of courage.

3. It is better to bear the chill of breaking up than the prolonged, daily discomfort of a relationship that has worn thin.

4. If you begin to feel as if you are chasing foxes, like a horse lathered from the hunt, ask yourself who is in the saddle. He who turns persons to prey has himself become ensnared in the hunt.

How to Propose to a Woman

*He who wants to succeed with
women must learn the difference
between a proposal and a proposition.*

I say, let her do it! By this I do not mean succumbing at the last possible moment to a barrage of seductive devices designed to rob you of your will. Quite the contrary, I mean to say: trust her sense of things, for in matters of the heart, most women are exceedingly capable. If we men have worked hard to know our minds, women have worked hard at knowing their hearts. A woman's declaration should be accepted in good faith: if she desired to take you against your will, she would be announcing her pregnancy, not her affection. Do not be put off by her proposal, for if a woman loves you, she can never be too forward. Have the courage, always, to say no if the match is not right. But also have the good grace to swallow false pride and say yes.

108

25 *On Marriage*

ood marriages are a mystery. You never find two alike, and for most you will be hard-pressed to explain what makes them succeed or not. I know only this: love is there somewhere—and lots of it. I expect if you follow the other advice I have given you, marriage will take care of itself, since I have never met a happily married man who was not at heart a good person.

Romance comes in all styles, in store-bought fashions, but marriage must be tailor-made, and each must sew for himself.

26

On Machines

ometimes I feel that machines are the most infernal things ever invented! I know they are thought to be the chief sign of civilization, but I cannot think that they alone measure man's progress. It seems to me the capacity to build massive industrial machines is no necessary sign of advancement, any more than a duel is a higher form than a brawl, simply because it employs fancy manufactured devices. To have discovered a more polite, efficient, and antiseptic way to kill another does not strike me as the height of civilized behavior. I would mark the more civilized man as one who has the common sense to dispense with a machine when it works evil.

The problem with a machine is that it cannot think for itself, though its mastery appears absolute in the appalling moment when you are depending on it and it fails. Moreover, there are a million things you do not know because another has made the machine. He knows its secrets and you are at his mercy. And once you have let his machine do your work, you become inclined to let him do your thinking as well. Until at last you depend on a proliferating mass of useless manufactures that rob you of your self-reliance as well as your income.

Since machines seem to be here to stay, I say to you only this: study them, use them, master them, calculate their cost, and make them do good. If you begin to crave them or worship them, you will lose both your bearings and your sense of well-being.

27

*When Nature was a woman,
she could take pity on us;
now that he is Science,
he is predictable and merciless.*

On Our Place in Nature

Nature has a power so immense we must hold it in awe if we properly appreciate it. If, in a despairing moment, you have given up all notions of religion, of good working in the world, of order working in your life, go out into the wilderness and be restored. Find an unspoiled spot and there you will find order, bountifulness, beauty that will take your breath away— and give it back to you refreshed. You cannot look on a primeval forest, with its majestic cathedral firs, and not believe there is a higher spirit at work! You have only to lie upon a beach amid sun and sand to have your cares dissolved with each wave of crashing surf. When your life becomes caught in the small, tangled webs of your own weaving, go out and study the grand design and your creative powers will be restored. When your life loses its vitality and meaning, consult the Maker of all things to find the power of the Life-force itself.

A return to Nature, if you go unarmed, taking only eyes to see and a humble spirit, will give you a sense of your place in the world. It is a special place, though somewhat smaller than man is inclined to believe, with his own inflated sense of pride and purpose. It is special because you have been given greater powers than most of God's creatures, powers that make you, know it or not, a custodian of the earth. So only as you care for the earth will it care for you. Each man must take up this trust if he is to be in tune with the world. And to be a worthy trustee, you must husband its wealth, not squander it like a profligate. Nothing makes you trust yourself more than the sense that all the earth is harmonious and balanced, and that your work has a peaceful, integral place in the ceaseless plan. Nothing will vex you more than the sense of confusion and disarray that comes from warring with Nature. Once you have fooled with the essential order of things, you will not be able to trust what will happen next. You will end up like a frustrated child with a pile of puzzle pieces: what began as a game ends in a test that makes you turn in tears to a Higher Intelligence. Do not join that pack of usurpers who scheme to steal the scepter and raise themselves to a higher place. Nature may be momentarily diverted but she is too powerful to be replaced. Instead, go out with quiet curiosity to study her ways, worship if you will, and make peace with her: she has a place for each of us.

28

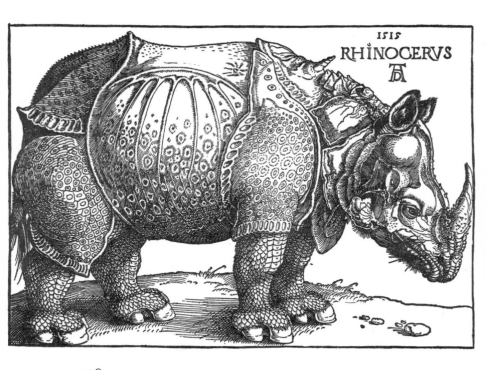

On Beauty

We have no better model of beauty than that provided by Nature. Even her ugliest creatures, the most bizarre bugs or beetles, are remarkably beautiful if you will dispense with first impressions and consider the handiwork. And it is no accident that artists since the beginning of time have taken the human body as the loveliest of forms. It is in fact an incredible creation. As complex as we are in function, you would be hard-pressed to imagine a form more economical and elegant.

You can do your body no greater favor than to respect its beauty and work in the most natural of ways to maintain its proportions. For this, regular exercise of a vigorous character is essential. No exhilaration exceeds that of a brisk swim in a chill mountain pond, a fine run through the fields, or the stretch and flex of muscles moving with catlike grace. Best of all, the regimen that maintains a finely tuned physique is also one that leaves you feeling wonderful within. Cultivate a taut, well-nourished body and you will possess beauty in two respects: a physical wholesomeness and radiance attractive to all, and an inner spirit that is happy because it is well housed. So, too, following the symmetry of all life, inner turmoil takes expression in ailments and disfigurement. If you are sick, fat, fatigued, it may be but a symptom and symbol of your inner state. Restore an inner alignment and your health can return as if by magic.

The principle of simplicity that lends Nature her beauty will also lend your life greater grace if you will adopt it as your axiom:

1. Be simple in dress, and you will never be out of style.
2. Select the simplest manner of expression and you will never be misunderstood.
3. Eat simple foods and they will always sit well on your stomach.
4. Seek the honest answer as the simplest and easiest, a lie being not only the wrong way but the *long* way to any worthy end.

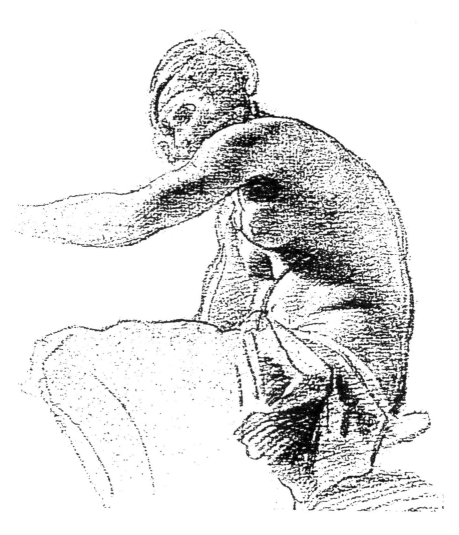

121

29

What to Do When the

ou will reach moments in life, as I have, when you will have utterly lost your way. Some external calamity may put you off the track, or you may suffer an internal confusion. In any case, it is a time for reflection, for collecting your resources, and for setting off in a new direction. I can recommend, as a strategy for containing the terror, that you take your upheaval as an occasion for new insight on what is really important in your life. Turmoil teaches us where we have gone wrong. Repose is our reward for courageously re-evaluating and rearranging our lives. Such storms of change can be weathered if you will keep these few things in mind:

Worst Happens

1. Return to first principles and trust those that are time-tested. Consult the legacy of culture, custom, and religion, though a wise and thoughtful man may discover his own unfailing laws.
2. Take regular food, rest, and recreation. This may seem trivial but it establishes the most essential order in your life. Optimism is not a matter of perspective so much as a matter of eating and sleeping well.
3. Depend on your friends. They are a great source of love, which in a moment of crisis is your most important resource of renewal. They are also

mirrors for seeing yourself more clearly when your own perspective has become clouded. They will help you to be accepting and to avoid the self-loathing that compounds crises.

4. Be honest with yourself and cling only to essentials. Many personal crises endure because we have not the courage to discard a cocoon we have outgrown.

5. A graceful life makes room for mistakes. Grace is no great metaphysical mystery; it is the capacity to walk well in life. But every new colt must stagger a bit before it finds its legs. It is by stumbling that we learn to look where we are going. We are born knowing how to cry, but not how to walk—this we must practice. Grace is giving ourselves a second chance, some time to learn. If you are generous with yourself, and patient, you will find your legs again and cultivate as well the faith that gives wings to transcend all obstacles in your path.

*Don't blame others:
the leaks may be
on their side of
the boat, but your side
will sink all the same.*

30 *And So, My Son...*

n all of this, I have tried to take those great watchwords of life—simplicity, truth, beauty, tolerance, love, discipline, integrity, courage—and make them more than pious words to hold in your mouth and sweeten your breath, that your neighbors may not be offended. I have tried to give them a practical content and show their merits as beacons for the inner journey. I have no doubt they shall express themselves in behavior that will bring approval from most; but my greatest hope is that they shall bring you to that precious place where you are at peace with yourself.

Farewell.